Tina D. Thompson

THE
ATTACK
ON
EVE

GOD'S VISION VS. WORLD'S VISION

ISBN 978-1-64458-615-0 (paperback)
ISBN 978-1-64458-616-7 (digital)

Christian Faith Publishing, Inc.
832 Park Avenue
Meadville, PA 16335
www.christianfaithpublishing.com

Printed in the United States of America

"Thompson communicates heartbreaking loss with strength and clarity in *The Attack on Eve*. Her message of faith and hope under such circumstance will challenge the reader to examine not only their own personal sorrows, but the sorrows of humanity in a world that seems all too willing to perpetuate the lies that materialism and walking in the ways of the world will bring the happiness we all seek. As Thompson explains, 'This walk in the absence of God's divine will, all too often leads to the opposite of everything women truly desire, the comfort and peace that the truth of God's Word provides.'

In this debut work of non-fiction, Thompson describes her experience of losing a child, and her climb from the depths of despair through a divine encounter. This encounter leads her to seek the guidance of scripture. The reader will accompany Thompson on this journey of revelation concerning the instability of our daily lives and families in turmoil because everyone is trying to live up to the expectations of a false narrative. Thompson's truth is our own truth because it is God's truth. Readers will not only enjoy the writing, they will walk away with a clearer perspective of this spiritual war we fight and the true enemy of our hopes and happiness. They will also see the salvation of God's word and the true love which comes from on high."

–Tabitha Prock, *Chicken Suze*

"This book is a concise, applicable, unique, dynamic conservative interpretation of scripture. It's a fresh openly at who is at fault and what may be done about it. Its focus is on the answer and not the negative self-pity approach. I truly appreciate the inspiration and insight of this study. It should be a personal desk guide for every serious pastor or any counselors dealing with the reality of life."

–Senior Pastor James Mason

Contents

Acknowledgments

*Give thanks in all circumstances; for this is the will
of God in Christ Jesus for you.*

—1 Thessalonians 5:18 (ESV)

A special thank you goes out to my wonderful husband Trevor and daughter Lilly who have encouraged and supported me during this book. I thank my parents, John and Charlotte Hunt, for raising me and taking me to church. My Aunt Ruth who always was there for me. Other acknowledgments are to Tom Bird for his wonderful teaching and coaching method and to all who prayed for me during this process. Thank you, Kerri Dill, James Mason, Tabitha Prock, Michael Garrett, Tonya Bruce, and David and Jeanette Smith for blessing me in so many ways. Finally, I thank the person reading this book for I know God has guided your decision on choosing my book. May God bless you during the reading. Thank you!

In my life, I spent too many days and nights dwelling on the hurt instead of the love God has for me.

Blessings of revelation, Tina D. Thompson

Introduction

I started off on this painful journey of soul searching some eight years ago. After my over-whelming loss of my son, I was a lifeless body. I spent three days in a barren garden covered with a haze of doom! I didn't bathe, speak, or eat. I tried to make sense of what happened or was happening to my life. I fought for the memory of my son, the feeling of him moving in my belly that felt like butter-flies in my stomach. I stared at the ultrasound photo of him until I had it memorized. I tried to keep him alive and fought my right to be a sad mother.

Amazingly, somehow through the desolation, I declared war on death and cried out to God in anger and hopelessness! "Is this your will for me, God? If you are the Prince of Peace, you need to come down and show me peace! Or I won't believe in you anymore."

Three nights later, around 3:00 a.m., I had a vision or a dream. I can't explain what I saw or experienced. All I know is that I was sitting in my navy recliner and suddenly my living room became a garden in front of me. It was so real and so beautiful! I was standing in front of a glistening gate which had a complete pearl with gold on the top and at the bottom. The design of the gate was so detailed with scrolled gold. The hinges and handle were made of gold. I felt myself glide toward the gate, and suddenly, the gate opened inwardly.

I was immediately floating in blue sky. I could see all around me and beneath, which was all blue, too. I saw a white blur getting closer and a man stood directly in front of me. He had light radiating from his head, his right side, and the palms of hands, and the tops of his feet. He didn't speak, but I could hear his voice in my head.

I couldn't take my eyes off him. His eyes were glistening with light. He looked to the right of himself and stretched out his right arm and immediately two, young adult males stood by him.

As he was still holding his right arm out to his side, he stretched out his left arm, and two more teenage boys appeared. He then turned to me and smiled with both arms stretched out to his side. I realized in that moment they were my sons! He spoke in my head with a calm voice to me, "I have your sons." Instantly, my heart was filled with complete hope. My pain was gone. I was restored back to my living room. I got up, took a shower, and ate. I was renewed.

I was told by many of people after my loss, "God will never give you more than you can handle." Somehow, this was supposed to make me feel better, but it made me mad. First of all, the only people who could really understand losing a child are those who have had it happen to them. You can't give more than you've experienced, period! There were the people who looked at me as if I was a freak of nature. They would ask if I had done anything to cause the babies to die. People assumed God was protecting them from this world and, in their warped way, that God was protecting the babies from me. People blamed me because I had sin in my life. Who doesn't have sin in their life?!

I realized in all of this confusion just to listen and believe in God. You see, people will let you down and talk about you. It's a part of the fall of man. Just like the serpent in the garden with Eve, I was in a garden with naysayers who would add and take away God's word, such as 1 Corinthians 10:13. In Paul's letter to the Corinthians, he wrote:

> No temptation has overtaken you that is not common to man. God is faithful, and he will not let you be tempted beyond your ability, but with the temptation he will also provide the way of escape, that you may be able to endure it. (1 Corinthians 10:13, ESV)

People quote this with intentions that God will not give you more than you can bear. They don't add that He will also provide the way of escape. This is what is helpful in times of need, as a way of escape from the grief, sadness, and depression. If in my despair, I didn't call out to God for an answer or hope to believe in Him, He would not have provided me with a way of escape through the vision of Him and my sons.

I learned my relationship with Him is the most important of all. I have to keep Him the centerpiece of my life. He and only He can give me peace. Of course, I'm not above anyone else in rank with Him, but I did get a breakthrough by calling out the honest words of my broken heart. "The Lord is near to the brokenhearted and saves the crushed in spirit." (Psalm 34:18) My favorite of the brokenhearted scriptures is, "The Spirit of the Lord God is upon me, because the Lord has anointed me to bring good news to the poor; He has sent me to bind up the brokenhearted, to proclaim liberty to the captives, and the opening of the prison to those who are bound." (Isaiah 61:1) Jesus quoted this scripture to his own people in Nazareth. They in turned rejected Him. He is our example of how to stand and proclaim God's written chapter that was written for Him for the appointed time. Jesus confirms that I am not the only person who has been rejected and experienced loss, and I won't be the last. I'm not alone. Once I understood this principle, I could move forward with a new chapter of my life. I learned to not care what people think or speak of me. My eyes were opened where theirs were not, and because of this understanding they didn't have the final say.

This scripture confirms that if I will continually follow Jesus and keep Him in the center of my garden, He will keep and help me write an amazing chapter to my life.

> For I know the plans I have for you, declares the Lord, plans for welfare and not for evil, to give you a future and a hope. Then you will call upon me and come and pray to me, and I will hear you. You will seek me find me, when you seek me with all your heart. (Jeremiah 29:11–13)

Most of the real golden nuggets in this book were my adventures to find what truly was my purpose in this garden of life. I've been fortunate enough to meet some amazing people, preachers, and teachers along my journey who have shown the light to my path with their God-given knowledge of God's Word, some through their own testimonies, and some just simple acts of kindness. Each person was orchestrated strategically by God to give me the channeling of God's love. For that I am grateful to God and give Him all credit.

As we navigate through today's garden, we must have the proper information and weapons of spiritual warfare to equip ourselves with knowledge and understanding of the Word. As you look at the chapters, please pause and reflect on your own life's experiences. There's a chapter to express every area of a person's life. The chapters can be used to speak into your life.

During the process of writing this book, I experienced loss, betrayal of friends/family, rejection, and was even mocked. I don't blame or even judge who have done these to me. I pray blessings of revelation for them to see Jesus's forgiveness and love for them. As Christians, we are encouraged through God's Holy Word to embrace change and to love one another. Please let us meditate on this scripture in Romans 12:9-21.

Let love be genuine. Abhor what is evil; hold fast to what is good. Love one another with brotherly affection. Outdo one another in showing honor. Do not be slothful in zeal, be fervent in spirit, and serve the Lord. Rejoice in hope, be patient in tribulation, be constant in prayer. Contribute to the needs of the saints and seek to show hospitality. Bless those who persecute you; bless and do not curse them. Rejoice with those who rejoice, weep with those who weep. Live in harmony with one another. Do not be haughty, but associate with the lowly. Never be wise in your own sight. Repay no one evil for evil, but give thought to do what is honorable in the sight of all. If possible, so far as it depends on you, live peaceably with all. Beloved, never avenge yourselves, but leave it to the wrath of God, for it is written:

"Vengeance is mine, I will repay," says the Lord.
To the contrary, "If your enemy is hungry, feed

him; if he is thirsty, give him something to drink;
for by so doing you will heap burning coals on
his head" Do not be overcome by evil, but overcome evil with good. (Romans 12:9–21)

This book uncovers the mysteries of the reasons we feel defeated and the emotional rollercoaster we sometimes experience. You'll learn where these attacks are coming from in this book. There are many clues you can discover in which you can recognize attacks. Solutions to attacks include biblical scriptures and solid testimonies. Everyone who has air in their lungs needs to know how to have spiritual warfare on the enemy, as the plot thickens in our own life stories, which brews daily. The old saying goes, "Knowing is half the battle." Really, it's the whole battle! We write our own life's story; we need to involve God in our lives every day, so He can give us a formula to write a new chapter.

The enemy is not creative; he simply uses relationships to destroy people. In fact, he twisted God's Word concerning the tree of knowledge of good and evil to make Eve second-guess or discredit God's Word. Who did she believe, her Creator or the counterfeiter? You will gain understanding on the motives of the enemy and why you feel so helpless at times. Your life will begin a new outlook on how to deal with conflict, hurt, loss, pain, and stress. So turn the page and begin today!

Chapter 1

World's Vision for Eve

But the serpent said to the woman, "You will not surely die. For God knows that when you eat of it your eyes will be opened, and you will be like God, knowing good and evil." (Genesis 3:4–5, ESV)

Imagine the first conversation between the serpent and Eve took place like this. "Look over here… what do you see? Come, come, come, let me treat you to a delicious fruit," said the serpent. The serpent being curious of Eve and noticed she was created different, and possibly he was jealous of her beauty. He realized she was the first of her kind. He was intrigued by her beauty. He knew what beauty was because he was made more beautiful than all the other angels. Lucifer was perhaps the most beautiful creation of God, maybe the most powerful of all the angels, and was called the bright morning star.

> *You had everything going for you.*
> *You were in Eden, God's garden.*
> *You were dressed in splendor,*
> *your robe studded with jewels:*
> *Carnelian, peridot, and moonstone,*
> *beryl, onyx, and jasper,*
> *Sapphire, turquoise, and emerald,*
> *all in settings of engraved gold.*

A robe was prepared for you
the same day you were created.
You were the anointed cherub.
I placed you on the mountain of God.
You strolled in magnificence among the stone of fire.
From the day of your creation you were sheer
*   perfection...*
and then imperfection—evil!—was detected in you.
In much buying and selling you turned violent, you
*   sinned!*
(Ezekiel 28:12–16, MSG)

In the beginning, Lucifer was a created being, he wasn't self-existent and now he no longer gives any light! Before God snuffed him out of heaven, He had everything going for him. He had the signature stamp of perfection on him! He was full of wisdom and was gorgeous. He was also in Eden. His covering was of gems and beautiful stones in a gold setting. He had bling! He had the first monogramming. Imagine an *L* on his shirt. Lucifer was the only recorded anointed angel. He sauntered on the mountain of God.

Well, that being said, this book was written because of the fall! The fall, as we know, is at the very moment Eve and the serpent communed. Let's set the stage for this scene. The serpent was resorting by the tree of knowledge of good and evil. Perhaps he was even dining from the tree or pretending to take a bite when Eve saw him. How did Adam and Eve get so close to the serpent? Was he in the shadow of the tree? Ezekiel 28:18 stated his appearance had changed when God "turns him to ashes on the earth in the sight of all who saw you." Did he whisper to them? Maybe he was talking to the tree, or maybe he was a fruit whisperer. Was it by surprise, or was it because he drew them in curiosity? Maybe he was having anger management issues because he was banished from heaven.

In Genesis 3:1, the serpent was categorized under the beasts of the field. In the scene when Adam and Eve are at the tree, the serpent could still walk, talk, and eat. His appearance was different from the angels they may have seen before. His approach was crafty, tempting, and suggestive. His first attack was on the tree. He was at the tree first, right? So what was he doing there? What drew them to the tree of knowledge of good and evil? Did the enemy think this tree would have a redemptive power or was it because he was already immortal? Was he only allowed to eat from this particular tree? We may never know the answers to these questions. It's interesting to imagine what was actually going on in the garden that day.

Thinking outside the box, angels were referenced in the Bible as males. Michael, Gabriel, Lucifer, and the angel of the Lord are described in the Bible. There are no references of female angels recorded. "For in the resurrection they neither marry nor are given in marriage, but are like angels of God in heaven." (Matthew 22:30, KJV) Angels are not human, so we shouldn't make assumptions they live and function in the same fashion humans do. Lucifer was speaking to a female for the first time and seeing a woman for the first time, he was in awe! He was used to males, since Adam was made in the image of God.

When Eve was created, Adam was asleep. He didn't see how God made her. She was made for him and to be his helpmate. Maybe the serpent thought she was a lesser form of man.

In the past, women weren't given much credit or respect. They were to produce good offspring and serve. Married women in biblical times to the early twentieth century who were barren often were ridiculed and scoffed at! It was shameful for the whole family. Women were viewed as not being a woman unless she gave birth. Some people even went as far as saying if a woman didn't have more than one, she was not a woman.

Times have really not changed in that sense, but women's equality has evolved a lot more. More women are choosing to wait years to decide on having children due to professional success or financial stability. This wait can cause infertility struggles. Today, doctors can test the husband and wife to figure out the reason for infertility. On occasions, it's the woman who may not be ovulating, an irregular menstrual cycle, thyroid disease, or the man has a low sperm count. Since birth control has been a part of preventing pregnancies, women feel they have control on the amount and time to produce or not produce at all. The world holds women to a high standard on producing offspring. Women can have power on childbearing. She can choose from several options: the pill, a condom, IUD, spermicides, abortion, etc.

Each year, millions of babies are born in the world. Every second, four babies somewhere in the world are born, however, around forty to fifty million abortions per year are performed worldwide. Every fourth unborn child is aborted! In America, there are four thousand abortions every day. It has been estimated that one in every four women has had an abortion. Females' childbearing age are all from this statistics. Why does the world's vision of women put great pressure to prevent, produce, or abort?

Some women choose to abort due to lack of money, not ready for the responsibility, and/or are unmarried. Since the world seeks self, let's look at the total picture. Warning: this may be hard to read! Okay, how did the woman get into the position of getting pregnant? It could have been a teen pregnancy, family incest, one night stand, or even a happily married woman. Was it consensual? Rape happens daily throughout the world. To prove rape, you need evidence through a proper doctor's exam (DNA test). According to www.kidshealth.org, rape is about power and is a crime.

Another world vision for us is self-image. The world wants and suggests young ladies to have a flawless appearance. Society expects us to be the perfect daughter, be well educated, be a strong leader, have a successful career, be the "breadwinner," marry later, be the perfect wife, experience childbirth later, be a perfect mom, keep the house clean, and make all meals from scratch. She's to be all that she can be and more. Being helpful with homework, PTA meetings, dance class, music lessons, sports, and Girl Scouts are to name a few more. She's also required to make sure all needs of her husband are met, listen about his day, laugh at his jokes, and iron his clothes. She's to be punctual at work and have emergency child care if snow or sicknesses arise. Think thin, think successful career, think supermom is today's vision for women. This vision starts as early as five years old!

Today, children mostly play with technology. Before the technology age, toys were the common choice. Today, social media, magazines, TV shows, and commercials send "attractive" messages. On average a woman views the Internet, social media, and TV shows seven hours daily. Unfortunately, she spends an average of thirty minutes with family. On top of competing with having time, comparison of body image follows. The average body fat of a lingerie model is eighteen percent or less. A healthy woman's body fat is around twenty-three to thirty-one percent. Let's consider that America's obesity rate is up. This is even more devastating to an overweight young lady. The world expects young ladies to be something that they can never achieve because of their own body type!

God's vision is for us to have inner beauty. He stated,

> Looks aren't everything. Don't be impressed with his looks and stature. I've already eliminated him. God judges persons differently than humans do. Men and women look at the face; God looks into the heart. (1 Samuel 16:7, MSG)

"He made us in His likeness, and we're created to serve Him with all our mind, soul, and strength." (Deuteronomy 6:5)

In the book of Esther, she gives us a wonderful example for us. She found favor with the king and he fell in love with her. She was granted beauty treatments, good food, and the best room the king could offer. Wow! Esther's inner beauty was seen when Mordecai commanded her to keep quiet about her people. She was put in custody of a man named Hegai. She didn't complain. Did I say she didn't complain? Let me say it again: Esther didn't complain. She asked for nothing when it was time to go to the king. She won the king's favor. She was submissive to authority.

Stop and chew on this: Mordecai suggested, "Who knows whether you have not come to the kingdom for such a time as this?" Esther replied with a total fast, nothing for three days. She submitted the finer things to gather the spiritual insight of God. Most women would stress eat, go on retail therapy (shopping), spin around on the floor. Her character was flawless! She showed remarkable strength during a turning point for the Jewish race. She drew to God for the answers. She believed in His understanding. She gained His favor by giving up the earthly king's provisions. She totally trusted God.

When you need a miracle the most, you'll believe the most! She didn't let her circumstance dictate her mindset. She continued in faith with fasting. Her influence was great with the others around her. She was proving self-discipline and self-control are important to turning the neck of God and the favor of man. He loves to see discipline plus trusting totally in Him to complete a mission.

Let's examine ourselves for a moment. Are we disciplined and self-controlled? Or are we continuing to circle through a revolving door every day of defeat? What's eating at you? The Word says, "Keep thy heart with all diligence; for out of it are the issues of life." (Proverbs 4:23, KJV)

Note: Fruit of the Spirit: Self-Control

Chapter 2

Devil's Suggestion

> The serpent was clever, more clever than any wild animal God had made. He spoke to the Woman: "Do I understand that God told you not to eat from any tree in the garden?" (Genesis 3:1, MSG)

Lucifer suggested a secret was kept from Adam and Eve to make them feel like they were missing out on something. This was the lie that the serpent told them. He wanted to create doubt. Doubt is the absence of faith. Faith is the hope of something that will come to pass. Doubt creates an atmosphere of uncertainty, frustration, and insecurity.

In my experience, doubt leaves a feeling of hopelessness! I used to seek other avenues to comfort my doubt. I would seek counsel from any one of my friends. My friends were not all believers. I was led astray by drinking of a different fruit because they didn't understand me or my situation. "So drink this, and it will help you forget your problem." The doctors did the same by prescribing mind-altering medications to help me stay in a partly cloudy mind with a chance of nightmare! The word *pharmacology* in classic Greek means "poison," and in modern Greek, it means "drug."

The power of suggestion comes from various mouths and body languages, tones, social media, e-mails, texts, and landlines. We live in a day and time were kids are so techie! Suggestions come in various forms to sway people's minds.

Let's start with Facebook, where a college student who wanted to connect college students through a common thread. What came of it? A billion-dollar revenue! A global social media was born. You can post about yourself either with texts, pictures, or videos. People can send you messages and posts. For example, if you received a message from someone who asked, "Are you single?" and you're married because of the personal info on your wall, you should be able to distinguish their intent, but let's say you're in a squabble with your spouse, or worse, pays you no attention, affection, nor adoration in days, months, or years. The power of this suggestion can be tempting to respond inappropriately if you choose to or not. It's totally an attack on marriage. This is the gateway of choosing faithfulness or infidelity.

Once you proceed in a direction away from the sacredness of marriage, consequences always follow choices! These consequences will have a major impact on your entire life, marriage, children, family, career, church, community, and health. Yes, I said community. People talk, listen to gossip, see things that we think they don't see, and repeat in a constant rotation.

If I told anyone about my unhappiness, that person is more likely to listen. Studies prove people remember the negative things and hold on to them more than the positive things. People in general compare their lives to others all the time. They're not always excited if good things happen to their friends. Jealousy in their hearts and thoughts are, "That's not fair," "Why not me too," and "Why do good things always happen to her and not me?" These flood their hearts. A wall builds between people and destroys the relationship. A healed heart lives in faith and love. "My flesh and my heart may fail, but God is the strength of my heart and my portion forever." (Psalm 73:26) Faith, hope, love, and charity springs out to others.

A person with a wounded heart has the opposite effects which are fear, doubt, unbelief, anger, hate, and rage. This in turn can suck the life out of people. They tear down people any way they can to make themselves feel better about themselves. We all have been there and had things happen to hurt us. We all have been broken and walked around wounded. We build towering walls to protect us from never getting hurt by anyone anymore. So the radar is out on the prowl for any negative information or flaws on people. So the so-called friend can say, "See, I told you she wasn't all that" and "I knew she wasn't good." No one has arrived to be perfect other than Jesus Christ. Everyone has fell short of the glory of God due to the fall of man. Redemption goes by knowing who you are in Christ and not what others think. It's what the truth of Jesus says about you! A good name is to be chosen rather than great riches. (Proverbs 22:1) The Reformation Study Bible footnote says a choice reputation is one of the social consequences of wisdom. In other words, choices do matter.

In surrendering to Christ, you win. You'll die to yourself and resurrect in the newness of life. (Romans 6:4) Those who know God's mercy must operate on the principle of mercy. If they don't show mercy but insist on justice, they won't receive mercy but justice. An unforgiving heart is subject to torments "until he/she should pay all." A truly forgiving heart is one result of spiritual rebirth (John 3:3) and "Be kind to one another, tenderhearted, forgiving one another, as God in Christ forgave you." (Ephesians 4:32)

Let us examine ourselves every day to see if we're living in the center of God's Will. The just shall live by faith (Galatians 3:11, KJV) and by every word that proceeds out of the mouth of God. (Matthew 4:4, Deuteronomy 8:3) If we are not reading the Word or spending time in prayer, we're not truly drawing closer with the Lord. (James 4:8) We're not perfect people, but we have a choice to forgive and repent, which means to turn away from our stinking thinking and stinking believing! "Wrecked, but not ruined" is an expression for a believer in Christ who's truly changed their life. What happens in a wreck? It's when two objects collide in an accident or on purpose. Sometimes we're standing in the exact spot where several wrecks collide, the question of fault feeds the fury of every collision.

Adam and Eve were standing near a tree where the greatest destroyer was! He was there to consume their soul, mind, and spirit. He was roaring with suggestions, but remember, they came up to him. What do you think he lured them with? Beauty, an aroma, or body language, but they made a choice to entertain his presence. He was suggestive!

Which fruit will you eat from? The Devil's or God's? It is still a choice for us today in our garden of Eden. The Bible warns, "Death and life are in the power of the tongue, and those who love it will eat its fruits." (Proverbs 18:21, ESV)

Note: Fruit of the spirit: Goodness

Chapter 3

Marriage Destruction

> So the Lord God caused a deep sleep to fall upon the man, and while he slept took one of his ribs and closed up its place with flesh. And the rib that the Lord God had taken from the man he made into a woman and brought her to the man. (Genesis 2:21–22, ESV)

The Lord God, who is such a loving father, presented a bride to Adam. He was pleased! He acknowledged where she came from when he said, "Bone of my bones and flesh of my flesh. Adam was given authority to call the beasts and birds." (Genesis 2:19–23) In his authority, he gave her the name Woman. Adam's conduct shows leadership and love by his words.

God conducts the first wedding with His words: "Therefore shall a man leave his father and his mother, and shall cleave unto his wife; and they shall be one flesh." (Genesis 2:24) The verbs *leave* and *cleave* are commands. The meaning of the word *leave* is "to abandon," and the word *cleave* means "to cling or stick to." God wants intimacy between a man and a woman. He illustrates to leave all you know and stick like glue to your woman. His plan for a man is to love and lead his supporting woman. The purpose of a woman is to be a supportive helper and respecter of her leading man. His blueprint to build a happy marriage is an attitude of surrendering all to each other.

According to the next passage, "And they were both naked, the man and his wife, and were not ashamed." (Genesis 2:25, KJV) The nudity appearance usually confuses many, but it's a symbol of cohesion. They were united by God and abided in His sovereignty and integrity. They enjoyed themselves without condemnation or disgrace. Adam and Eve lacked concern to be open to an attack. They lived fearless, shameless, and blameless.

Until one day, they met the craftiest beast of the field. The serpent spoke to them, and Eve spoke back. This opened a gate for influence of doubt as the serpent pressed on the issue of restriction, and Eve forgot about all the other trees freely given to them. (Genesis 2:16) The serpent highlighted the only tree to change the course of God's plan for the newlyweds. Adam remained silent. (Genesis 3:6) Eve discussed the prohibition and embellishes God's Word by saying not to even touch it. (Genesis 3:3) She was in conversation with the father of lies. (John 8:44) He started influencing by his consistent attack of words. He opposed God's Word by telling Eve, "You will not surely die." (Genesis 3:4)

Eve felt like she was missing something, that God was holding out and not giving them all the garden, or to become as God. (Genesis 3:5) Eve lusted for the fruit and had a desire to rebel. Allowing this emotion to take over, she reacted. The serpent instigated Eve to sin, which made a domino effect for Adam to sin. (Genesis 3:6) They knew to do the right thing, but completely did the opposite. They didn't fall into sin by accident, but they chose to eat to it. The blindness of sin changed them to the opened door of sin. The serpent crafted an unfinished painting to Adam and Eve. He twisted the truth and only gave what would change Eve's mind to that of the serpent's.

> And the man said, "The woman whom You gave to
> be with me—she gave me [fruit] from the tree, and
> I ate." (Genesis 3:12, AMP)

So today, where does this bring us to Adam and Eve in the garden? They are no different from newlyweds starting out. They had everything they needed, but as soon as they got on their own into the world, problems came. The battle of words and wills.

Adam and Eve had seen the tree of knowledge of good and evil many times before they had an encounter with the serpent. Why did it now appeal to Eve more? Why did Adam respond by blaming Eve? Why did Adam not speak to the enemy "beast" since he had been given authority? The attack is with an inquisitive question from the serpent, which began marriage destruction between God, Adam, and Eve.

The serpent pursued and persuaded Eve to rethink about the tree. Eve responded with, "Neither shall ye touch it, lest you die." This was not what God instructed. He said, "But of the tree of the knowledge of good and evil you shall not eat, for in the day that you eat of it you shall surely die." (Genesis 2:17) Another word for acceptance is silence. In other words, Adam didn't dispute it he just ate the fruit without questioning Eve. They both ate of the forbidden tree.

Eventually, Adam and Eve will age and deteriorate. They will not remain as God had intended, pure and holy. They will be separated from God, just as the serpent was separated from God. The serpent's influence changed the lives of Adam and Eve, as well as their offspring!

Influential words have consequences. The consequences last longer than the influences and words because it is the outcome of the influences and words from the company you keep. The company you keep will be the person you become. This legendary phrase has been said throughout the years. It is true. If you surround yourself with worldly and ungodly people who speak only of worldly and ungodly things, then you'll become a product of them. The influence is peer pressure, which in turn has power over your thinking. If you choose to allow yourself to associate with these influential people, you'll fall into their ways of thinking, speaking, and habits. The influential person or persons will have control of you. It's a form of bullying!

Nevertheless, people don't always like taking responsibility for their actions. When God asked Adam, "Where are you and who told you you're naked?" Adam responded by blaming. So Adam is the inventor of the blame game! Eve retaliated and blamed the serpent. The serpent was probably enjoying the show. I could imagine he was laughing at God's creation as they were trying to squirm out of their sin.

Of course, judgment followed. It had to. God's word is true and just. "For the Lord reproves him whom he loves, as a father the son in whom he delights." (Proverbs 3:12, ESV)

God's vision for man and woman is to turn to Him for answers, and to not lean on their own or someone else's understanding. He has provided a way through Jesus to make it possible to communicate with Him directly. If He can speak to Jesus directly, He can also speak to you directly. You have to seek Him and His kingdom first. (Matthew 6:33) This is the beauty of free will. It was the same way with Adam and Eve in the Garden of Eden. They had a choice. They could have walked away or spoken God's Word to the serpent. For example, "It is written that we should not eat from the tree of knowledge of good and evil, so take that, serpent. Because God said it, I believe it." No, instead they went on their free will and thought they were missing out, then judgment came.

World's vision is to seek anyone, but God's advice. The counselors, psychologists, mediums, astrologists, and fortune-tellers have made their business in getting in everybody's business. They're usually in it for the money. No person can do what only Jesus can do for them. No person is perfect like our God! Consistently, people will let you down and disappoint you. In our unstable world, we put so much stock in what people say and do that we miss the opportunity to be still and listen to God. This is why so many marriages are destroyed. A man and a woman in a marriage who seek counsel from an ungodly source are unwise. The Bible states:

> Blessed is the man who walks not in the counsel
> of the wicked, nor stands in the way of sinners,
> nor sits in the seat of scoffers; but his delight is
> in the law of the Lord, and on his law he medi-

ates day and night. He is like a tree planted by streams of water that yields its fruit in its season, and its leaf does not wither. In all that he does, he prospers. The wicked are not so, but are like chaff that the wind drives away. Therefore, the wicked will not stand in the judgment, nor sinners in the congregation of the righteous; for the Lord knows the way of the righteous, but the way of the wicked will perish. (Psalms 1:1–6)

I love this illustration of the tree planted by streams of water. It reminds me of the garden of Eden. In essence, to have a happy marriage, avoid evil influences, evil deeds, and evil attitudes. A married couple who holds on to God's Word will prosper and be happy.

Happy! What makes a happy marriage? Seeking counsel from God, not others. Even if the others are walking with the Lord, they are still human. They have sin in their lives and will pass judgment either with words or thoughts. "The counsel of the Lord stands forever, the plans of his heart to all generations." (Psalm 33:11)

Husbands and wives are to blame for seeking world's counsel. They watch reality shows to see what to do next. They read books on many topics of self-help. Only a few people read the Word of God. Why?

Let's examine this verse:

But understand this, that in the last days there will come times of difficulty. For people will be lovers of self, lovers of money, proud, arrogant, abusive, disobedient to their parents, ungrateful, unholy, heartless, unappeasable, slanderous, without self-control, brutal, not loving good, treacherous, reckless, swollen with conceit, lovers of pleasure rather than lovers of God, having the appearance of godliness, but denying its power. Avoid such people. For among them are those who creep into households and cap-

ture weak women, burdened with sins and led
astray by various passions, always learning and
never able to arrive at a knowledge of the truth.
(2 Timothy 3:1–7)

The real reason people don't read the Word is because they're too busy doing everything else than to be still and know their creator. The enemy is still busy seeking out who he can destroy. He only flees when we speak God's Word to him. Remember when Jesus was in the wilderness and fasting. The enemy came to visit him and tried to get him to sin. Jesus was in the wilderness, not a garden. Jesus told him, "It is written" several times, and Satan left. Little word of God produces little faith, and a lot of word of God produces a lot of faith. It's really that simple.

God put many things on the earth for us not to taste. If it were not so, we wouldn't have free will. He's the creator of all flesh and blood. It's important not to give yourself over to just anyone, so they won't take over your strength. The moment Eve opened the door to the serpent, she was the first to partake in communion with the serpent and opened her mouth to sin first. You see, the serpent has a clock and agenda, too! He wants to destroy as fast as he can anything pertaining to godliness. He hates anything resembling our Creator. The enemy wants to keep you tormented and in constant sin. He's a counterfeiter and the author of lies. He doesn't create anything, but chaos and war!

The garden of Eden is a real place. Today, it's hidden from our naked eye because of their sin and the exile of Adam and Eve. Their marriage was rocky after the fall! I'm sure the blame game continued and make-up sessions occurred. This produced the offspring Cain and Abel. The saga continued with the jealousy and murder of Abel. The cracking of edges in their marriage continued. The blame and guilt came in again. It continues again and again like a revolving door. How did they handle the pain and loss of Abel? How did they overcome?

Today, it's the same pain within any marriage due to a loss of a child. In the Bible, there's no record of their actions or words. It would be silly to think they didn't react to the tragedies. Adam and Eve not only lost their son Abel, but their son Cain. He had to leave and separate himself from them.

A separation brings isolation and temptations. It can be the final straw to keep loved ones to reconcile. Married couples who separate will be more likely to divorce than couples who seek out God's will for their marriage. Couples who take in their own hands the separation will fall into more temptation and sin. They will allow their friends or family to influence their way of thinking and believing. On the other hand, if there's sound, godly friendships and family influences, the couple has more of a chance. Eventually, the separation will show the true character of the couple, the intent of not giving up and caving in on a marriage of selfishness and miscommunication. In order to reconcile, the couple has to be in an agreement to communicate in person, not texting, e-mails, and other electronic methods. It's the responsibility of both to try! Family members who meddle in the affairs of the couple should be stopped by the mutual agreement of the couple. "It is an honor for a man to keep aloof from strife, but every fool will be quarreling." (Proverbs 20:3, ESV)

If children are involved, it should be conducted in privacy. The children will be broken the most! The selfishness of the parents shouldn't consume them to get their children involved, nor made to take sides or be put in any situation where decisions are to be made. Children are not experienced in life to make such painful decisions. They have the right to have a good childhood. Parents should keep them protected, as if there was a fire in the house to keep them safe. The fire of our words should be put out around them.

> And the tongue *is* a fire, a world of unrighteousness. The tongue is set among our members, staining the whole body, setting on fire the entire course of life, and set on fire by hell. (James 3:6, ESV)
>
> There is one whose rash words are like sword thrusts, but the tongue of the wise brings healing. (Proverbs 12:18)

This verse is so true. Seeking God's will for everything and leaning on Him for wisdom and understanding instead of our own. It's easy to say, but hard to implement.

In essence, what destroys a marriage? A thought of lack, a choice to betray, and an absence of responsibility are seen in Genesis 3. Today is no different from the time of Adam and Eve for the opportunity to express free will. We all have thoughts and choices. The prophet Malachi states that none should be faithless to the wife of his youth and that God hates divorce. (Malachi 2:15–16, AMP) We must choose well.

Here are some examples of marriage destruction downfalls:

1. Financial lack
2. A choice to betray (an adulterous affair)
3. A thought of lack or missing out (comparison to other people's lives)
4. Perception of spouse (a spouse may change in attitude, appearance, and attributes)
5. A loss of a child/children or a rebellious child/children
6. Pure selfishness (A spouse may have sickness or job loss, which either a spouse decides to abandon the marriage. A spouse is completely consumed with self-worth and self-centeredness.)
7. Lack of communication (not taking time for each other)
8. Addictions (sex/pornography, drugs, alcohol, gambling, sports [obsession with golf, football, basketball, etc.])
9. Physical, verbal, and emotional abuse
10. Hidden feelings (A spouse retaining baggage of resentment, being unforgiving, anger, envy, jealousy, and hate.)
11. Criminal past (A spouse withholds his/her past criminal convictions.)
12. Secret friendships (A spouse may entertain past/present boyfriends/girlfriends either in person, social media, or phone calls in secret.)

13. In-laws (A spouse may allow in-laws to meddle in their marriage.)
14. Incest (A family member who commits a sexual crime either with a parent, child, sibling, or grandchild.)

All of these horrific attacks on a marriage can happen! Marriage can be extremely difficult when bad choices are chosen.

On the other hand, to prevent most of these, the Bible recommends to chose a spouse of the equal yoke. A biblical principle in 2 Corinthians 6:14–18, Paul is discussing to separate believers from unbelievers. He's concerned with the worldly and ungodly influences mingling with believers.

> Don't be unequally yoked with unbelievers. For what partnership has righteousness with lawlessness? Or what fellowship has light with darkness? What accord has Christ with Belial? Or what portion does a believer share with an unbeliever? What agreement has the temple of God with idols? For we are the temple of the living God, as God said:
>
> "I will make my dwelling among them
> and walk among them,
> and I will be their God,
> and they shall be my people.
> Therefore go out from their midst,
> and be separate from them, says the Lord,
> and touch no unclean thing;
> then I will welcome you,
> and I will be a father to you,
> and you shall be sons and daughters to me,
> says the Lord Almighty."
>
> (2 Corinthians 6:14–18, The Reformation Study Bible, ESV)

God gave Eve to Adam to take as his helpmate. In Genesis 2:21–22, God took one rib to make woman. He became a donor and a husband at the same time. He gave something up for her. He gave so that she may live. He gave blood, bone marrow, and nourishment to her. They are of the same kind.

In my Hebrew self-study through friends and relatives, I've learned that God is a god of order. He likes numbers. I also studied and practiced dental hygiene for several years and learned anatomy and physiology in college. My background knowledge has helped me understand orders and functions.

The ribs are located on the chest, which houses the lungs, the heart, and other vital organs. Male and female both have twelve pairs. In the Hebrew language, twelve means divine government. Also, there are seven ribs that are called true ribs. Seven is the number for completed perfection. I like to think on Jesus's truth as perfect completion! Also the number one means in the beginning. If we put them together, in the beginning, God completed perfection with Adam and Eve, and He set their marriage on divine government. He told them, "Be fruitful and multiply and fill the earth and subdue it, and have dominion over the fish of the sea and over the birds of the heavens and over every living thing that moves on the earth." (Genesis 1:28)

In essence, He said, "I give you control and manage what I have given you." He trusted them. He allowed them to think for themselves and make their own decisions. Until the encounter with the serpent, which in turn caused influence and sin to enter the lives of Adam and Eve and their offspring's future.

Today, we're still living in the sin of our first parents. We have choices to make every day. We can choose among different varieties of fruit of many trees today. There are still trees to be avoided. The tree of lust, the tree of flesh, and the tree of selfishness, but the fruit of the spirit you can enjoy abundantly!

Paul explains, "Wives, submit to your own husbands, as to the Lord. For the husband is the head of the wife even as Christ is the head of the church, his body, and is himself its Savior." (Ephesians 5:22–23, ESV) As wives, we are to respect and allow our husbands to lead us.

"Husbands, love your wives, as Christ loved the church and gave himself up for her." (Ephesians 5:25, ESV)

True love's greatest example is Jesus Christ. He showed His love by His self-sacrifice for all sinners. "Greater love has no one than this, that someone lay down his life for his friends." (John 15:13, ESV)

We must mediate on the truths of God's Word day and night for our marriages. We must not allow the enemy one second of our precious time. We must confess our sins and be clean in our hearts to keep loving our spouses.

> Hatred stirs up strife, but love covers all offenses.
> (Proverbs 10:12, ESV)

> Above all, keep loving one another earnestly, since love covers a multitude of sins. (1 Peter 4:8, ESV)

Note: Fruit of the Spirit: Love

Chapter 4

Parental Relationship with Eve

> As arrows are in the hand of a mighty man; so are children of the youth. (Psalm 127:4, KJV)

God sees our children as arrows of deliverance. They're not just here to be entertained, be a fashion trendsetter, or to just procreate grandchildren. He knew our children before we had them. "For you formed my inward parts; you knitted me together in my mother's womb." (Psalm 139:13, ESV) The enemy wants to destroy our arrows/children before they're out of the quiver/womb!

In the biblical days, babies were put through the fire, thrown to the crocodiles, or slain in the arms of their mothers. Today, it's a business. Instead of praying for a bare womb, they use abortion for birth control.

If only they realized; God is in control! He will listen to the prayers of those who want nothing to do with a child as well as those who want them.

> My people are destroyed for lack of knowledge; because you have rejected knowledge, I reject you from being a priest to me. And since you have forgotten the law of your God, I also will forget your children. (Hosea 4:6, ESV)

Parents direct the pathway of the arrows, whether the direction is right or wrong. "Train up a child in the way he should go: and when he is old, he will not depart from it." (Proverbs 22:6, KJV) Our arrows will go in one direction. When the setting of the arrow is weak, the direction will be weak. The direction won't be precise. The arrow's destination will not be fulfilled. On the other hand, if parents set the bow with skillfulness and strength, the arrow will reach its potential destination.

Blessings and curses can be said over you and your child/children. Words are powerful! You can rest assured that one drop of Jesus' blood will change the curse that has been said over you. He can turn a curse into a blessing! "But the LORD your God would not listen to Balaam; instead the LORD your God turned the curse into a blessing for you, because the LORD your God loved you." (Deuteronomy 23:5, ESV). Every battle that is given to Him, He will deliver you. He will cover you with His feathers!

> He shall cover thee with his feathers, and under his wings shalt thou trust: his truth shall be thy shield and buckler. Thou shalt not be afraid for the terror by night; nor for the arrow that flieth by day. (Psalms 91:4–5, KJV)

Remember, God will keep those who desire to be kept. Whatever thorn is in your side is what God is trying to change in your life or in your child's life.

God put many things on the earth for us to exercise our free will. He is creator of all flesh and blood. Just like the garden of Eden, God has orchestrated options for his children to choose from. These options are called choices. We must be knowledgeable and methodical not to give ourselves over to just anyone or anything, so they won't take over our strength. Remember He looks at the intentions of our hearts.

Adam and Eve produced their arrows outside the garden of Eden: Cain and Abel. Their transgression of a fallen nature was transferred to their children. Adam and Eve lost their self-control at the tree of knowledge of good and evil. Their lack of submission to God put in motion the negative consequences to future generations.

God planted His seed in Adam, which follows us today. Cain was the first seed of Adam and, unfortunately, he didn't heed to the instruction of obedience. Even though God himself interceded on Cain's behalf, Cain used his freewill to further the fall of man.

As Cain left to create himself a new life, he also had his memories still with him. He was created with emotions to experience life as God intended. One of these emotions was sadness. Sadness is the most mischievous of spirits and the worst to the servants of God. A man/woman who uses sadness to control other people is in dire need of God's Word. They're dangerous to be around! They can destroy the spirits of all who are around them. They can suck the life out of people just dealing with them. It's selfish and an easy out to use false sadness as a defense mechanism!

In the scriptures, Jesus uses analogies to help people understand his teachings. Good vines (believers) can be choked by the weeds (nonbelievers) by evil words. Nonbelievers (weeds) trust their own opinions and judgments (have many for others) and only believe in themselves. Good vines (believers) trust God's way and will. On the other hand, trusting in Him brings and increases wisdom and understanding in life. Not trusting in Him brings increased worry, stress, anger, hardship, sickness, and death. "The human spirit can endure a sick body, but who can bear a crushed spirit?" (Proverbs 18:14, NLT)

Let's examine this: if a nonbeliever is stressed, they may give up and faint in their day of adversity. They might isolate themselves from the problem, person, or world. Adam and Eve did when they sinned in the garden. They hid from God. Satan wants to rob you of your life and fast! "The thief comes only to steal and kill and destroy. I came that they may have life and have it abundantly." (John 10:10, ESV)

The Holy Spirit cannot work when dwelling in self-pity. It grieves the Holy Spirit because doubting took place first and not the Word. The person puts more emphasis on themselves. The Word Jesus and the Holy Scriptures are the first and utmost importance. No Word plus no faith equals no results. It's an insult to the Holy Spirit if you doubt. The devil will always contradict the Word. Christians have too much to praise Jesus for to allow themselves to be tricked by the devil to believe; He can't bring them out. Just as He brought the children of Israel out of the bondage of stressful slavery, He will bring today's believer out if they will trust, obey, and believe He can. Jesus said, "Let not your hearts be troubled. Believe in God; believe also in me." (John 14:1)

> When I find someone who will commit their life to me, I will bless their life through a thousand generations. "He remembers his covenant forever, the word that he commanded, for a thousand generations." (Psalm 105:8)

When God saved you, it was not only about you; it was multigenerational!

> For no good tree bears bad fruit, nor again does a bad tree bear good fruit, for each tree is known by its own fruit. For figs are not gathered from thorn bushes, nor are grapes picked from a bramble bush. The good person out of the good treasure of his heart produces good, and the evil person out of his evil treasure produces evil, for out of the abundance of the heart his mouth speaks. (Luke 6:43–45, ESV)

We're all guilty of being hung by our own tongues! Who could ever say they are innocent, but Jesus. He is our true vine.

> I am the true vine, and my Father is the gardener. He cuts off every branch in me that bears no fruit, while every branch that does bear fruit he prunes so that it will be even more fruitful. You are already clean because of the word I have spoken to you. Remain in me, as I also remain in

you. No branch can bear fruit by itself; it must remain in the vine. Neither can you bear fruit unless you remain in me. I am the vine; you are the branches. If you remain in me and I in you, you will bear much fruit; apart from me you can do nothing. If you do not remain in me, you are like a branch that is thrown away and withers; such branches are picked up, thrown into the fire and burned. If you remain in me and my words remain in you, ask whatever you wish, and it will be done for you. (John 15:1–7, NIV)

We must trust in His Word and not our own. We need to change what or who we listen to and what we watch. We must adjust our habits for our future generations. It will produce better relationships with our children, children's children, and children's children's children.

Death and life are in the power of the tongue, and those who love it will eat its fruits. (Proverbs 18:21)

Note: Fruit of the Spirit: Patience

Chapter 5

Kid Disobedience

Even a child makes himself known by his acts,
by whether his conduct is pure and upright.
(Proverbs 20:11, ESV)

Before heaven and earth were created, only God existed. He in his great power and imagination orchestrated the cosmos, and in it he developed heavenly hosts known as angels. "You are the Lord, you alone. You have made heaven, the heaven of heavens, with all their host, the earth and all that is on it, the seas and all that is in them; and you preserve all of them; and the host of heaven worships you." (Nehemiah 9:6, ESV)

"In the beginning God [prepared, formed, fashioned, and] created the heavens and the earth." (Genesis 1:1) "By faith we understand that the worlds [during the successive ages] were framed [fashioned, put in order, and equipped for their intended purpose] by the word of God, so that what we see was not made out of things which are visible." (Hebrews 11:3)

Well, I like to think they are God's kids, and some of His kid's behaved disobediently! The first disobedient son was Lucifer. Angels were commanded to be created. (Psalm 148:5) After the heavens and the earth were made, there rose a problem in heaven. It was a dispute among angels.

How art thou fallen from heaven, O Lucifer, son of the morning! How art thou cut down to the ground, which diest weaken the nations! For thou hast said in thine heart, I will ascend into heaven, I will exalt my throne above the stars of God: I will sit also upon the mount of the congregation, in the sides of the north: I will ascend above the heights of the clouds; I will be like the most High. (Isaiah 14:12–14, KJV)

Lucifer was a beautiful and anointed cherub. He saw himself handsome and wise. He allowed himself to be convinced he could obtain what was God's. He was jealous and envious. He wanted the spotlight! At that time, lying was never heard in heaven. The angels abode with great confidence in God's cherub, Lucifer. Lucifer began whispering twisted truths about God and boasted about himself. He changed the angels' minds and views of God. In John 8:44, Jesus describes him, "You are of your father the devil, and your will is to do your father's desires. He was a murderer from the beginning, and does not stand in the truth, because there is no truth in him. When he lies, he speaks out of his own character, for he is a liar and the father of lies." As a result of his lies, Lucifer began a war in heaven!

Now war arose in heaven, Michael and his angels fighting against the dragon. And the dragon and his angels fought back, but he was defeated, and there was no longer any place for them in heaven. And the great dragon was thrown down, that ancient serpent, who is called the devil, and Satan, the deceiver of the whole world—he was thrown down to the earth, and his angels were thrown down with him. (Revelation 12:7–9, ESV)

The son was cast out. What was his sin? It was pride.
In Proverbs, Solomon lists six character flaws God hates:

A proud look [the attitude that makes one over-estimate oneself and discount others], a lying tongue, and hands that shed innocent blood, a heart that creates wicked plans, feet that run swiftly to evil, a false witness who breathes out lies [even half-truths], and one who spreads discord (rumors) among brothers. (Proverbs 6:17–19, AMP)

The fear of the Lord is hatred of evil. Pride and arrogance and the way of evil and perverted speech I hate. (Proverbs 8:13, ESV)

In the pride of his face the wicked does not seek him; all his thoughts are, "There is no God." (Psalm 10:4, ESV)

Let the lying lips be put to silence; which speak grievous things proudly and contemptuously against the righteous. (Psalm 31:18, KJV)

Finally, "For all that is in the world—the desires of the flesh and the desires of the eyes and pride of life—is not from the Father, but is from the world. And the world is passing away along with its desires, but whoever does the will of God abides forever." (1 John 2:16–17, ESV)

Now that we have covered what caused the first sin, we can understand more as to why disobedience is so prevalent. Looking for clues in the Bible, there are five kids who stand out: Cain (pride of life), Ham (lust of the flesh), Samson (lust of the eyes), Absalom (pride of life), and Hophni and Phinehas (lust of the flesh).

Cain is the most famous disobedient kid in history. He was the first kid born in the world!

And Adam knew Eve his wife; and she conceived, and bare Cain, and said, I have gotten a man from the Lord. (Genesis 4:1, KJV)

Cain was a tiller of the ground. He brought an offering of fruit of the ground to the Lord. On the other hand, his brother Abel brought a living sacrifice for his sins. Cain became jealous of Abel because God liked Abel's offering better. God came to Cain in love to ask why he was so sad and upset. God gave Cain a chance through his conversation and advice to do well or the consequences if not. Cain chose first to talk with Abel, then in the heat of the discussion, he killed Abel.

God visited Cain again. He asked Cain, "Where is your brother?"

Cain responded, "I don't know, and I don't keep up with him!" He lied to and disrespected God all in one statement.

God said, "I hear the voice of your brother's blood crying to me!"

God then curses the ground that Cain tills, so that the ground will not yield her strength. God called him a fugitive (wanderer) and a vagabond (homeless person).

Cain responded with, "That is too much for me. I can't handle it!" He was only thinking of himself. Notice no remorse for killing Abel due to hate in his heart. He could only think of his situation he then said, "Well, I'm a wandering homeless person now, and someone will kill me!"

Again, the Lord came to Cain with compassion and concern saying, "Not so! If anyone kills Cain, vengeance shall be taken on him sevenfold." God put a mark on Cain to protect him so that no one who met him would kill him. (Genesis 4:1-15, MSG)

Cain left all he knew and started fresh in Nod, which is east of Eden. "He drove out the man, and at the east of the garden of Eden he placed the cherubim and flaming sword that turned every way to guard the way of the tree of life." (Genesis 3:24)

Cain returned to the spot where his parents were driven out of the garden. Cain found a wife and built a city. He named his son and city Enoch. Through his descendants, his wickedness prevailed. That holds true,

> Lamech said to his wives: "Adah and Zillah, hear
> my voice; you wives of Lamech, listen to what
> I say: I have killed a man for wounding me, a
> young man for striking me. If Cain's revenge is

sevenfold, then Lamech's is seventy-sevenfold."
(Genesis 4:23–24)

Once again, history is repeated. Cain had a choice, and he was warned by the Father. Just as his parents disobeyed, Cain followed in disobedience.

After the great flood, Noah began to be a man of the soil, and he planted a vineyard. He drank of the wine, became drunk, and laid uncovered in his tent. Ham was one of the three sons of Noah. "He saw the nakedness of his father and told his two brothers outside." (Genesis 9:20–22, ESV)

Unfolding Ham's sin, we can see he knew his father was drunk as he lay in his tent. Ham saw his father's nakedness, and then he told his brothers. Noah's privacy was invaded by Ham choosing to look at his nakedness. It wasn't an accident. He intentionally looked at him. He then told his brothers about it. He wanted them to take ownership for some of what he did, he bragged about seeing him, or he gossiped about his father's body. Either way, he was guilty of the lust of the flesh. When Noah woke up, he knew what had happened and cursed Ham's son Canaan, not Ham. Ham was the youngest of Noah's sons, and God had already blessed Ham. Noah knew the curse would have to be on his youngest grandson, Canaan.

"The land of Ham" was referred in Psalms 105:23,27, 106:22, and 1 Chronicles 4:40. In Genesis 10:6–20, The Reformation Study Bible, ESV, we see the names of Israel's most dreaded enemies: Egypt, Philistia, Assyria, and Babylon. Sodom and Gomorrah are also under Ham's lands and nations. Nimrod was a grandson of Ham. He was a mighty hunter and the builder of the Tower of Babel. Nimrod's name means "we shall rebel" in Semitic root. In ancient times, people named their child according to their character. The personality of Nimrod is how the Semitic root MRD has been used, even into our own time. The Ancient Semitic root MRD (marad) is the origin of our words MaRauDer and MuRDer.

Unfortunately, history repeated itself. If only Ham would have chosen to be obedient, the repercussions would have been a blessing on his son Canaan, but he chose disobedience.

Samson is a great example of a disobedient kid. He had a problem with the lust of the eyes. One day, Samson's mother was visited by an angel. An angel of the Lord appeared to his mother and told her she would have a son, and he would be a Nazirite, which means to be separate from the world. She was instructed not to drink wine/strong drink and to not eat anything unclean. When Samson grew to a young man, he told his father, "Get her for me, for she is right in my eyes." (Judges 14:3, ESV) Israelites were not to marry with foreigners. (Deuteronomy 7:3–4, ESV) Before Samson met his wife, he encountered a lion, and Samson tore it apart. His power was from the Lord. He was instructed to not go near a dead body. (Numbers 6:6) He didn't listen to the guidance from his parents, so he journeyed on his own way. As the Bible reads, "Then he went down and talked with the woman, and she was right in Samson's eyes." (Judges 14:7, ESV) His parents also inquired why he couldn't find a woman among his people, instead of the Philistines.

Samson's saga continued with killing thirty men after his first wife gave his secret riddle away to save herself and her family. When Samson learned of his wife's betrayal, he then set foxes on fire, destroyed olive orchards, and stacked grains. (Judges 15:5) The people of the town came to capture him for the Philistines. He agreed to have his hands bound by new ropes and took to the Philistines. (Judges 15:12–14) The ropes could not hold him. He killed one thousand Philistines with a fresh jawbone of a donkey. (Judges 15:15) Samson continues to touch dead carcasses and falls into more disobedience.

Samson didn't waste any time. He traveled to Gaza and saw a prostitute. (Judges 16:1, ESV) He didn't honor his parents' request. (Judges 14:2–4, ESV) Samson again met another woman named Delilah, who was money hungry. Delilah was bribed by the Philistines to get Samson's secret. Samson caves in and tells her the secret to his strength; his hair. The Philistines gouged out his eyes and took him to prison. (Judges 16:21) This is very ironic due to his problem with the lust of the eyes. Samson is forced to walk in circles to grind mill. In time, his hair began to grow back and his magnificent strength returned. Samson was created to save Israel from the Philistines, instead he immersed himself into their culture. Ultimately, God's Word came to pass even though Samson was disobedient. Samson called on God to help get his strength back to avenge the Philistines one last time. Samson pushed the two pillars that the house rested and begged God to "let me die with the Philistines." (Judges 16:30) God granted his request.

Samson was a God-given powerhouse! He had a hard time listening and learned the hard way. He also had a hot temper. He was a womanizer, murderer, liar, thief, vandal, and riddler. He chose disobedience.

Hophni and Phinehas were guilty of lust. They were the sons of Eli the high priest. They were priests themselves. (1 Samuel 1:3) The Bible calls them worthless men. "They did not know the Lord." (1 Samuel 1:12) They would consume the fat of the offerings, and if the people wouldn't give it to them, they would take it by force. "The sin of the young men was very great in the sight of the Lord, for the men treated the offering of the Lord with contempt." (1 Samuel 2:17)

"Their father, Eli, was very old, and he kept hearing all that his sons were doing to all Israel, and how they lay with the women who were serving at the entrance to the tent of meeting." (1 Samuel 2:22) "They would not listen to the voice of their father, for it was the will of the Lord to put them to death." (1 Samuel 2:25)

The Lord brought a man to Eli to explain the disobedient consequences. "Why then do you scorn my sacrifices and my offerings that I commanded for my dwelling, and honor your sons above me by fattening yourselves on the choicest parts of every offering of my people Israel?" (1 Samuel 2:29) Eli failed in controlling his sons and allowed their evil works to continue. Their choice of disobedience to the Lord caused death to come to all three of them, and the Ark of the Covenant was captured in the hands of the Philistines. (1 Samuel 4:10–11) They chose disobedience.

King David had many sons. Absalom was the third son of David. His mother was Maacah, the daughter of Talmai, king of Geshur. (2 Samuel 3:3) Now in all Israel, there was no one so much to be praised for his handsome appearance as Absalom. From the sole of his foot to the crown of his head, there was no blemish in him, and when he cut the hair of his head (for at the end of every year he used to cut it; when it was heavy on him), he weighed the hair of his head, two hundred shekels (five lbs) by the king's weight. (2 Samuel 14:25-26)

Absalom had a sister named Tamar. When his sister Tamar was violated by their half-brother Amnon, Absalom hated him! He waited two years to get vengeance, then he fled to his grandfather's land in Geshur and lived there three years. (2 Samuel 13:38) His grandfather was the king of Geshur. Absalom came back to Jerusalem and lived separate from where his father King David lived. (2 Samuel 14:24)

Absalom waited two years without coming to see his dad, King David. He sent for Joab (a mighty man of King David's) twice to send him before the king, and Joab refused. Absalom sought out vengeance on Joab's land and he set it on fire. (2 Samuel 14:28–30)

Finally, Absalom met with his father. He soon took a chariot and horses, and fifty men before him. (2 Samuel 15:1) He quickly conspired against his dad to steal the hearts of men of Israel. (2 Samuel 15:6) David is then forced to leave Jerusalem. Absalom decided to ask his advisor for help.

> Then Absalom said to Ahithophel, "Give your counsel. What shall we do?" Ahithophel said to Absalom, "Go in to your father's concubines, whom he has left to keep the house, and all Israel will hear that you have made yourself a stench to your father, and the hands of all who are with you will be strengthened." So they pitched a tent for Absalom on the roof. And Absalom went in to his father's concubines in the sight of all Israel. (2 Samuel 16:20–22)

Absalom has lost his way even more and decides to kill his father.

> Next Ahithophel advised Absalom, "Let me handpick twelve thousand men and go after David tonight. I'll come on him when he's bone

tired and take him by complete surprise. The whole army will run off and I'll kill only David. Then I'll bring the army back to you—a bride brought back to her husband! You're only after one man, after all. Then everyone will be together in peace!" (2 Samuel 17:1-3, MSG)

Sadly, Absalom was the one caught up in an oak tree by his head and was killed by Joab with three darts.

And Absalom happened to meet the servants of David. Absalom was riding on his mule, and the mule went under the thick branches of a great oak, and his head caught fast in the oak, and he was suspended between heaven and earth, while the mule that was under him went on. And a certain man saw it and told Joab, "Behold, I saw Absalom hanging in an oak." Joab said to the man who told him, "What, you saw him! Why then did you not strike him there to the ground? I would have been glad to give you ten pieces of silver and a belt." But the man said to Joab, "Even if I felt in my hand the weight of a thousand pieces of silver, I would not reach out my hand against the king's son, for in our hearing the king commanded you and Abishai and Ittai, 'For my sake protect the young man Absalom.' On the other hand, if I had dealt treacherously against his life (and there is nothing hidden from the king), then you yourself would have stood aloof." Joab said, "I will not waste time like this with you." And he took three javelins in his hand and thrust them into the heart of Absalom while he was still alive in the oak. (2 Samuel 18:9–14, ESV)

Unfortunately, Absalom died before his time. He had good looks, fame, and riches, but he wanted the throne at all cost! He was a narcissistic arson with a passive-aggressive personality. Absalom was guilty of pride of life. He chose disobedience.

We've discussed five sons who were given life on this earth. Some were born in royalty and priesthood. Others were born to save a nation. They all failed and died before their time. They chose a path without God's will. Today, path choices are still God's will or world's will. It's our choice to choose.

On the other hand, we as parents can guide kids' thoughts, and it will bring an inheritance of a lifetime. The way we speak around them and treat them matters. Parents can shepherd their hearts by being present.

Peter was instructed by Jesus to feed his sheep and to suffer not the little children to come unto him. (Matthew 19:14) We can make sure we're bringing our children to a spirit-filled, Bible-reading, and believing church. We can pray with our children daily, praying in the fruits of the spirit, which is love, joy, peace, long-suffering, gentleness, goodness, faith, meekness, temperance: against such there is no law. (Galatians 5:22–23, ESV) We can pray for their future spouses and offspring. We can teach them to be independent such as Hannah, mother of Samuel, taught him at a very early age, and it stuck with him for a lifetime. (1 Samuel 1:24–28) When we're obedient, God is exalted.

> Train up a child in the way he should go; even when he is old, he will not depart from it. (Proverbs 22:6)

> Apply your heart to instruction
> and your ears to words of knowledge.
> Do not withhold discipline from a child;
> if you strike him with a rod, he will not die.
> If you strike him with the rod,
> you will save his soul from Sheol.
> My son, if your heart be wise,

my heart too will be glad.
My inmost being will exult
when your lips speak what is right.
Let not your heart envy sinners,
but continue in the fear of the Lord all the day.
Surely there is a future,
and your hope will not be cut off.
(Proverbs 23:12–18, ESV)

If you do well, will you not be accepted? And if you do not do well, sin is crouching at the door. Its desire is contrary to you, but you must rule over it. (Genesis 4:7, ESV)

Children, obey your parents in the Lord, for this is right. "Honor your father and mother" (this is the first commandment with a promise), "that it may go well with you and that you may live long in the land." (Ephesians 6:1–3, ESV)

For all who are led by the Spirit of God are sons of God. For you did not receive the spirit of slavery to fall back into fear, but you have received the Spirit of adoption as sons, by whom we cry, "Abba! Father!" The Spirit himself bears witness with our spirit that we are children of God, and if children, then heirs—heirs of God and fellow heirs with Christ, provided we suffer with him in order that we may also be glorified with him. (Romans 8:14–17, ESV)

Note: Fruits of the Spirit: Kindness and Gentleness

Chapter 6

Work Confrontation

And the Lord God took the man and put him into the Garden of Eden to dress (work) it and to keep it. (Genesis 2:15, KJV)

Adam was placed in the garden with the company of birds, fish, and animals. God decides to bring every beast of the field and every fowl of the air to Adam to see what he would call them. (Genesis 2:19) God was helping him use his dominion, but he was missing something. His own kind. So out of the graciousness of God's heart, He made him a helper.

Adam called her woman and later Eve. Eve wasn't named until she became a mother. (Genesis 3:20) Eve's work title was mother. She gave birth to Cain and Abel. Cain's work title was tiller of the ground and Abel's work title was sheep keeper. One day, a heated work conflict happened among them. Jealousy and envy began to brew in Cain's heart when he compared his offering to Abel's. God showed compassion as well as leadership to talk to Cain to channel his emotions in the right direction. Cain chose his way. Inevitably, the family relationship was destroyed as well as two lost workers for Adam and Eve.

Another example of work confrontation is between Jacob and Laban. Here's a little background of Laban's family tree. He was the brother of Rebekah. She married Isaac, Abraham's son. She gave birth to twin boys, Esau and Jacob. Laban was the uncle to Esau and Jacob. They were first cousins to Leah and Rachel, Laban's daughters.

Prior to Jacob fleeing his homeland, his mother devised a heist to steal Esau's blessing from Isaac. Jacob gets the stolen blessing and flees to Laban. Ironically, Laban tricks Jacob in working for Rachel's hand in marriage for seven years, but Laban's intention was to give Leah to him instead. Jacob discovers the manipulation the morning after his wedding. He works another seven years and gets to finally marry Rachel.

A seasoned shepherd, Jacob had knowledge as to how to increase the flock by breeding the flock to produce stronger off-spring. Jacob wanted to leave and be independent from Laban's pastures. Jacob confronts Laban. Laban responds, "If I have found favor in your sight, I have learned by divination that the Lord has blessed me because of you. Name your wages, and I will give it." (Genesis 30:27–28)

With a greedy heart, Laban saw the blessing, and he wanted to manipulate the Lord through Jacob to serve his own greed. Jacob said to him, "You yourself know how I have served you, and how your livestock has fared with me. For you had little before I came, and it has increased abundantly, and the Lord has blessed you wherever I turned. But now when shall I provide for my own household also?" (Genesis 30:29–30)

Laban still cheated after the work confrontation, but Jacob was blessed even more by God. Now Jacob heard that the sons of Laban were saying, "Jacob has taken all that was our father's, and from what was our father's he has gained all this wealth." (Genesis 31:1) Jacob decided to take action by gathering his wives for a staff meeting in the field. He said, "You know that I have served your father with all my strength, yet your father has cheated me and changed my wages ten times." (Genesis 31:6–7)

Laban changed his mind on how he was paying him with the flock many times. Remember, he did the very same thing with his daughters when he promised them to Jacob. Jacob explained his case to his wives, and they agreed to be in allegiance with Jacob. They left without telling Laban. Laban found them and confronted Jacob as to why he left with all of his daughters and grandchildren and stole his gods. Jacob answered Laban,

> I was afraid. I thought you would take your daughters away from me by brute force. But as far as your gods are concerned, if you find that anybody here has them, that person dies. With all of us watching, look around. If you find anything here that belongs to you, take it." Jacob didn't know that Rachel had stolen the gods. (Genesis 31:31–32, MSG)

Now Jacob didn't know that Rachel had stolen them. Laban barged in on Rachel to find his precious idols. He didn't find them. By now, Jacob had enough!

> What is my offense? What is my sin, that you have hotly pursued me? For you have felt through all my goods; what have you found of all your household goods? Set it here before my kinsmen and your kinsmen, that they may decide between us two. (Genesis 31:36–37)

Notice that Jacob gets witnesses on both sides which show his leadership. Jacob then summarizes his cause.

> These twenty years I have been with you. Your ewes and your female goats have not miscarried, and I have not eaten the rams of your flocks. What was torn by wild beasts I did not bring to you. I bore the loss of it myself. From my hand you required it, whether stolen by day or stolen by night. There I was: by day the heat consumed me, and the cold by night, and my sleep fled from my eyes. These twenty years I have been in your house. I served you fourteen years for your

two daughters and six years for your flock, and you have changed my wages ten times. If the God of my father, the God of Abraham and the Fear of Isaac, had not been on my side, surely now you would have sent me away empty-handed. God saw my affliction and the labor of my hands and rebuked you last night. (Genesis 31:38–42)

Laban defended himself:

The daughters are my daughters, the children are my children, the flock is my flock—everything you see is mine. But what can I do about my daughters or for the children they've had? So let's settle things between us, make a covenant—God will be the witness between us. (Genesis 31:43–44, MSG)

So they agreed to cease from arguing of matters and belongings, but disagreed on the name of the treaty. Finally, Laban agreed to name the agreement the same as Jacob; Galeed, which means a heap of witness.

During this work confrontation, character flaws were highlighted. Deception, greed, selfishness, secrets, strong wills, and tempers were among the flaws. Laban wanted Jacob to stay so he would do all the work. Laban collected all the profit, so he had to change the wages because Jacob would make all the profit. He was greedy and conniving!

Jacob had discernment. He saw the truth and wanted out of it. In the end, Laban had no remorse for using Jacob to gain wealth. Jacob realized that his help came from the Lord.

Several years later, Joseph was one of the twelve sons of Jacob. He was in several work confrontations. First, his brothers hated him for reporting to their father because they were not at the correct work site. His brothers were shepherds, and Joseph was sent to bring a report back to their father. In essence, he was keeping tabs on them.

The brothers were not where they should have been. Joseph found them in Dothan. (Genesis 37:17)

On one occasion, Jacob made Joseph a coat of many colors, which made them hate him, and they couldn't speak peacefully to him anymore. After that, God gave Joseph a dream, and when he told it to his brothers, they hated him even more. (Genesis 37:4) Joseph had another dream and was rebuked by his father. His brothers were more jealous of him, but his father kept the saying in mind. (Genesis 37:11)

When his brothers saw him coming, they secretly conspired against him.

> Here comes this dreamer. Come now, let us kill him and throw him into one of the pits. Then we will say that a fierce animal has devoured him, and we will see what will become of his dreams. (Genesis 37:19–20)

They chose not to kill him, but they sold him! He was purchased by Potiphar, an officer of the Egyptian Pharaoh. Potiphar noticed he had favor with the Lord. Joseph was promoted over all the household and prospered well. (Genesis 39:1:6)

The brothers needed a story to tell the father, so they took Joseph's colorful coat, and covered it with blood to present it to their father. This is ironic in itself. Jacob and his mother Rebekah used goatskin to pretend to be Esau to steal Isaac's blessing. The brothers told Jacob that Joseph was killed by a wild beast. They wanted to steal and end Joseph's favor.

The Bible describes, Joseph was handsome in form and appearance. Potiphar's wife wanted him to be her lover, and he responded by, "How can I do this great sickness and sin against God." (Genesis 39:9) She kept tempting him, and he ran! She lied to her husband and made a story up about Joseph raping her. (Genesis 39:17–18) Potiphar had to respond and he placed Joseph in prison.

While in prison, Joseph was in charge of all the prisoners. (Genesis 39:22) Joseph noticed two new prisoners one day. He asked,

"Why are your faces downcast today?" They said to him, "We have had dreams, and there is no one to interpret them." (Genesis 40:8) Joseph asked if he could help. He knew what it was like to dream dreams and have the untold mystery lingering in his thoughts. He requested to be remembered if he interpreted the dreams accurately. "Only remember me, when it is well with you and please do me the kindness to mention me to Pharaoh, and so get me out of this house." (Genesis 40:14) This was his soon-to-be ticket out of jail!

Two years later, Pharaoh had a dream. He needed someone to interpret it. The cupbearer remembered, and Pharaoh fetched Joseph. Joseph's God-given ability to interpret dreams allowed him to be promoted to governor of Egypt.

During the drought predicted by Pharaoh's dream, Joseph's brother came to buy grain. They didn't recognize him, but he recognized them. Joseph tested them to see how they would respond to adversity. He wanted them to bring Benjamin to him. The brothers brought him, and Joseph exposed his true identity to them.

> Joseph said to his brothers, "Come near to me, please," and they came near. He said, "I am your brother, Joseph, whom you sold into Egypt. And now do not be distressed or angry with yourselves because you sold me here, for God sent me before you to preserve life. For the famine has been in the land these two years, and there are yet five years in which there will be neither plowing nor harvest. And God sent me before you to preserve for you a remnant on earth and to keep alive for you many survivors. So it was not you who sent me here, but God. He has made me a father to Pharaoh and lord of all his house and ruler over all the land of Egypt." (Genesis 45:4–8, ESV)

In this example of Joseph's brothers, they displayed jealousy and hatred. The brothers felt less than in their father's eyes, which made them jealous. Joseph was an overseer of them, and he kept a close eye on them because his father told him to. His brothers were older than he, and if he told on them, it made him look like a tattletale. Although, he brought honest reports.

Joseph wanted to share and communicate with his brothers, but it only made them hate him. He was called names and was gossiped about by his brothers. The jealous rage sent him into a pit and sold to Ishmaelites.

Joseph became an overseer of Potiphar's house. One day, he was tempted to have an affair with the lady of the house, and he chose to run! This showed Joseph to be faithful to God and to Potiphar. She lied, and Joseph was called a rapist. He was thrown into prison and soon became overseer of the prisoners. While he was in prison, he was given a gift of interpretation of dreams, which allowed him to get to the throne room and interpret the Pharaoh's dream. This was God's final overseeing career for Joseph. He was to rule over Egypt and be the breadwinner for the world.

Another man of God, put through the fire was Daniel. He was no stranger to adversity. He was plotted against by his coworkers to be fired. The scripture writes,

> Then the presidents and princes sought to find occasion against Daniel concerning the kingdom; but they could find none occasion nor fault; forasmuch as he was faithful, neither was there any error or fault found in him. Then said these men, we shall not find any occasion against this Daniel, except we find it against him concerning the law of his God. (Daniel 6:4–5, KJV)

So they conspired together to have the king sign a petition. The petition was if anyone makes a petition to any god or man for thirty days, except to you, O king, shall be cast into the den of lions. (Daniel 6:7) So the king signed the petition. His coworkers/conspirators went to the king after they spied on Daniel praying three times a day. They ran to the king and reminded him of the petition he signed and asked the king to follow through with the consequence.

The King had no choice, but to throw Daniel into the lion's den because of his prayer life and faith in God. Daniel explains, "My God sent his angel and shut the lion's mouths, and they have not harmed me, because I was found blameless before him; and also before you, O king, I have done no harm." (Daniel 6:22, ESV) Their plot back-fired on the coworkers and their families. They were found guilty and thrown into the lion's den and killed. (Daniel 6:24)

Again another set of rivals, Mordecai and Haman, were cowork-ers. Haman was promoted and set his throne above all the officials who were with him. All the king's servants who were at the king's gate bowed down and paid homage to Haman, for the king had so com-manded concerning him, but Mordecai did not bow down or pay homage, and when they spoke to him day after day and he wouldn't listen to them, they told Haman, in order to see whether Mordecai's words would stand, for he had told them that he was a Jew. When Haman saw that Mordecai didn't bow down or pay homage to him, Haman was filled with fury. (Esther 3:2–5)

Haman was a proud man and demanded respect! He plotted against Mordecai and the Jews. He persuaded the king to make writ-ten letters to be posted against the Jews. To destroy all Jews, young and old, women and children, in one day, the thirtieth day of the twelfth month, which is the month of Adar (February–March), and to plunder their goods. (Esther 3:13–14) He went to great lengths to have Mordecai and the Jews annihilated!

To his own surprise, God had chosen a vessel in the king's bed-room who had his favor. God used the beauty and gentle spirit of Esther, Mordecai's niece, to save her people, the Jews. Haman was hung on the gallows intended for Mordecai.

Today, working with people can be a challenge. Everyone is unique in all of their ways. We come from different backgrounds and geographies. Because of these differences, they can bring misun-derstandings as what seems normal to one may seem crazy to others. Miscommunications and emotions can be a nightmare! Here's the solution: have good communication to eliminate conflicts.

In a perfect world such as the garden of Eden, a conflict can still occur. The serpent recommended the fruit to Adam and Eve, which had conflict all over it. They were tricked. It can still happen today. People still lie, plot, and conspire against coworkers every day.

In conclusion, leadership is crucial to minimize conflicts. Secondly, the leader must enforce behavior boundaries. What is the acceptable behavior allowed and what is not? This should be clear to all employees. It should be oral and written knowledge to them. Thirdly, if a conflict arises, it should be dealt with immediately! A conflict is always worth resolving. Finally, a leader can use a work confrontation or conflict to teach lessons for the involved parties. Leaders can learn mindsets and tendencies of the coworkers, which can help diffuse later conflicts. Leaders making all efforts to do the right thing will help lead others to do the right thing.

Paul said it best on how a Christian should walk in love. He makes it crystal clear, but when the test comes our way, at times it's hard to follow through. Please be encouraged by this passage:

> Now this I say and testify in the Lord, that you must no longer walk as the Gentiles do, in the futility of their minds. They are darkened in their understanding, alienated from the life of God because of the ignorance that is in them, due to their hardness of heart. They have become callous and have given themselves up to sensuality, greedy to practice every kind of impurity. But that is not the way you learned Christ!—assuming that you have heard about him and were taught in him, as the truth is in Jesus, to put off your old self, which belongs to your former manner of life and is corrupt through deceitful desires, and to be renewed in the spirit of your minds, and to put on the new self, created after the likeness of God in true righteousness and holiness. Therefore, having put away falsehood, let each one of you speak the truth with his neighbor, for we are members one of another. Be angry and do not sin; do not let the sun go down on your anger, and give no

opportunity to the devil. Let the thief no longer steal, but rather let him labor, doing honest work with his own hands, so that he may have something to share with anyone in need. Let no corrupting talk come out of your mouths, but only such as is good for building up, as fits the occasion, that it may give grace to those who hear. And do not grieve the Holy Spirit of God, by whom you were sealed for the day of redemption. Let all bitterness and wrath and anger and clamor and slander be put away from you, alone with all malice. Be kind to one another, tenderhearted, forgiving one another, as God in Christ forgave you. (Ephesians 4:17–32, ESV)

You shall love the Lord your God with all your heart and with all your soul and with all your mind. This the great and first commandment. And a second is like it: You shall love your neighbor as yourself. (Matthew 22:37–39, ESV)

Note: Fruit of the Spirit: Faithfulness

Chapter 7

Church Destruction

He has told me, O man, what is good;
and what does the Lord require of you
but to do justice, and to love kindness,
and to walk humbly with your God?
(Micah 6:8, ESV)

Scripture creates a fact, not a feeling! If we choose to follow the instruction manual, the Holy Bible, we'll hide the Word in our hearts that we might not sin against God. (Psalm 119:11) By choosing to repent (changing mind) and confessing (acknowledge) our sins, or what I like to say, "Run to the mercy seat, and it will cleanse us of our crooked thinking, believing, and living," we will live the scripture in a fact, not a feeling! When your thinking lines up with the thinking of God, our lives will straighten up with the Word of God.

When you decide to follow Jesus and make Him lord of your life, you become a Christian. It's a choice. It's a name we call ourselves who confess our sins and repent to our Lord Jesus Christ. "For God so loved the world, that he gave his only Son, that whoever believes in him should not perish but have eternal life." (John 3:16, ESV) We're convicted of our sins and convinced the only way is through Jesus. "For all have sinned and fall short of the glory of God." (Romans 3:23, ESV) We believe He died for our sins by His death on the Cross and His resurrection. "He personally carried the load of our sins in his own body when he died on the cross so that we can be finished with sin and live a good life from now on. For his wounds have healed ours." (1 Peter 2:24, TLV) We allow Him to be Lord of our lives. We pray to Him. We tithe to Him.

> Honor the Lord with your wealth and with the first fruits of all your produce; then your barns will be filled with plenty, and your vats will be bursting with wine. (Proverbs 3:9–10, ESV)

When we love God, we will love giving.

> Bring the full tithe into the storehouse, that there may be food in my house. And thereby put me to the test, says the Lord of hosts, if I will not open the windows of heaven for you and pour down for you a blessing until there is no more need. (Malachi 3:10, ESV)

We do this in a love and obedience to Him.

> But to all who did receive him, who believed in his name, he gave the right to become children of God, who were born, not of blood nor of the will of the flesh nor of the will of man, but of God. (John 1:12–13)

The church is the "body of Christ" of whom are born-again believers who congregate together to worship the "head," which is Jesus. "And he is the head of the body, the church. He is the beginning, the firstborn from the dead, that in everything he might be preeminent." (Colossians 1:18)

The birth of the church was after the ascension of Jesus. The day of Pentecost came when the believers received the Holy Spirit. "But you will receive power when the Holy Spirit has come upon you, and you will be my witnesses in Jerusalem and in all Judea and

Samaria, and to the end of the earth." (Acts 1:8 ESV) The believers assembled themselves together in devotion to worshipping the Lord.

> When the day of Pentecost arrived, they were all together in one place. And suddenly there came from heaven a sound like a mighty rushing wind, and it filled the entire house where they were sitting. And divided tongues as of fire appeared to them and rested on each one of them. And they were all filled with the Holy Spirit and began to speak in other tongues as the Spirit gave them utterance. (Acts 2:1–4)

The Holy Spirit is the guidance and influence of the church.

> And they devoted themselves to the apostles' teaching and the fellowship, to the breaking of bread and the prayers. And awe came upon every soul, and many wonders and signs were being done through the apostles. And all who believed were together and had all things in common. And they were selling their possessions and belongings and distributing the proceeds to all, as any had need. (Acts 2:42–45)

Love, selflessness and harmony were the characteristics for the first church. "And the Lord added to their number day by day those who were being saved." (Acts 2:47)

Soon, the ugly headed enemy would show up and cause adversity. "But the high priest rose up, and all who were with him [that is, the party of the Sadducees], and filled with jealousy they arrested the apostles and put them in the public prison." (Acts 5:17–18) God gave an open door for the church members and provided a way of escape, "But the angel of the Lord by night opened the prison doors and brought them forth and said, 'Go, stand and speak in the temple to the people all the words of this Life.' (Acts 5:19–20) They obeyed the angel of the Lord.

A man named Gamaliel, a Pharisee and teacher of Saul/Paul, advised to let the apostles have space.

> So in the present case I tell you, keep away from these men and let them alone, for if this plan or this undertaking is of man, it will fail; but if it is of God, you will not be able to overthrow them. You might even be found opposing God!" So they took his advice, and when they had called in the apostles, they beat them and charged them not to speak in the name of Jesus, and let them go. (Acts 5:38–40)

High priests were common in the Bible choosing to make ungodly decisions. Such as Aaron, the first appointed priest. When Moses was on the mountain with God, Aaron complied with who wanted a statue to worship.

> So Aaron said to them, "Take off the rings of gold that are in the ears of your wives, your sons, and your daughters, and bring them to me." So all the people took off the rings of gold that were in their ears and brought them to Aaron. And he received the gold from their hand and fashioned it with a graving tool and made a golden calf. (Exodus 32:2–4)

Another example, Eli and his sons were priests who chose to be disobedient to the commandments of God, "And he said to them, "Why do you do such things? For I hear of your evil dealings from all people." (1 Samuel 2:23, ESV)

Jesus even taught about the ungodliness of priests. "For you shut the kingdom of heaven in people's faces. For you neither enter yourselves nor allow those who would enter to go in." (Matthew 23:13)

He added later in the teaching, "For you are like "whitewashed tombs, which outwardly appear beautiful, but within are full of dead people's bones and all uncleanness." (Matthew 23:27)

Caiaphas and the council used Judas to sell out Jesus, "Then the chief priests and the elders of the people gathered in the palace of the high priest, whose name was Caiaphas, and plotted together in order to arrest Jesus by stealth and kill him." (Matthew 26:3–4, ESV)

Our true enemy, Satan, uses the same tactics as he did in biblical times. He is not creative, but he is destructive. He delegates personalities to execute his crafty demises. He is thrilled when he uses the godly positions of individuals to disgrace and discredit the church.

> But false prophets also arose among the people, just as there will be false teachers among you, who will secretly bring in destructive heresies, even denying the Master who bought them, bringing upon themselves swift destruction. (2 Peter 2:1, ESV)

Now we understand the church destruction can brew within the church itself. The enemy is here to trip us all up! He is a serpent! So what can we do to defend the church? We need to be proactive and know who our enemy is. Who are we at war with? The devil!

> Be sober minded; be watchful. Your adversary, the devil, prowls around like a roaring lion, seeking someone to devour. Resist him, firm in your faith, knowing that the same kinds of suffering are being experienced by your brotherhood throughout the world. (1 Peter 5:8–9)

We can learn to pray as followers to God to understanding our weaknesses. Asking God to shine light on them can be humbling, but necessary if you're serious to be the body. "For everyone who asks receives, and the one who seeks finds, and to the one who knocks it will be opened" (Luke 11:10). Make a list of your weaknesses. Be specific and brutally honest. If you have a trustworthy prayer warrior/warriors to help you pray, seek them out. "For where two or three are gathered in my name, there am I among them." (Matthew 18:20)

Reading the Word of God every day is cleansing for the church to review their mercies and receive proper guidance. It's a detoxification of worldly influences.

> This Book of the Law shall not depart from your mouth, but you shall meditate on it day and night, so that you may be careful to do according to all that is written in it. For then you will make your way prosperous, and then you will have good success. (Joshua 1:8, ESV)

Christians outlasting the adversity must remember who gave us the Word!

> All Scripture is breathed out by God and profitable for teaching, for reproof, for correction, and for training in righteousness, that the man of God may be complete, equipped for every good work. (2 Timothy 3:16–17)

Serving one over sitting to be served must be the attitude of the church. We must initiate an outreach to help, heal, and harvest. As we sow into the church, we will reap the benefits of the Holy Spirit.

> It shall not be so among you. But whoever would be great among you must be your servant, and whoever would be first among you must be your slave, even as the Son of Man came not to be served but to serve, and to give his life as a ransom for many. (Matthew 20:26–28)

We must be unified. We are to be in fellowship and love one another. He paid a costly price that we could never pay on our own.

> Come, I will show you the Bride, the wife of the
> Lamb. (Revelation 21:9)

Note: Fruit of the Spirit: Peace

Chapter 8

Overcome by the Blood of the Lamb and the Word of Testimony

> And they overcame him by the blood of the
> Lamb, and by the word of their testimony;
> and they loved not their lives unto the death.
> (Revelation 12:11, KJV)

The world's system cannot be trusted nor relied on to succeed. Please remember to take no thought for your life. "Therefore do not be anxious about tomorrow, for tomorrow will be anxious for itself. Sufficient for the day is its own trouble." (Matthew 6:34, ESV) God's kingdom is to last for all eternity. In America, our government writes laws/bills on paper made of wood. Moses wrote laws on stone tablets, but Jesus came to fulfill the law. "Do not think that I have come to abolish the Law or the Prophets; I have not come to abolish them but to fulfill them." (Matthew 5:17)

Detaching yourselves from the world system and attaching yourself to God's system will increase your ability to achieve a better relationship with God. "Draw near to God, and he will draw near to you. Cleanse your hands, you sinners, and purify your hearts, you double-minded." (James 4:8) By doing so, you can take authority of lack and fear. Be of good cheer, for the Lord is with us! He has not forsaken us! In the world you'll have tribulations, and we must respond in faith. He will be our deliverer and our peace, because He overcame with the shedding of His precious blood, and we overcome by the word of our testimony.

His blood applied to our hearts will speak! The Lord said, "The voice of your brother's blood is crying to me from the ground." (Genesis 4:10) How much more does the blood of Jesus speak over you? The blood of Jesus works to appease the one true living God.

> Whom God put forward as a propitiation by his blood, to be received by faith. This was to show God's righteousness, because in his divine forbearance he had passed over former sins. It was to show his righteousness at the present time, so that he might be just and the justifier of the one who has faith in Jesus. (Romans 3:25–26, ESV)

God looks at the heart and not the outward appearance as man does.

> But the *Lord* said to Samuel, "Do not consider his appearance or his height, for I have rejected him." The *Lord* does not look at the things man looks at. Man looks at the outward appearance, but the *Lord* looks at the heart. (1 Samuel 16:7, NIV)

Man looks at the heart as an organ that pumps blood through the body, but he isn't looking for the intentions of the heart. The heart is the highlighted area for God! He is looking for the blood of His Son! God wants to hear from our hearts, "It is finished." The only good in us is the blood of the Lamb and our testimony. Jesus is the Lamb of God. John the Baptist said it, "Behold, the Lamb of God, who takes away the sin of the world!" (John 1:29)

On the other side, It is the "bull's eye" for the enemy to see that we are God's child. It makes us a target! The red blood of Jesus in the middle of our chest illuminates His power and presence.

Sin is what separates man/woman from God. It puts us in a stranglehold of bondage. We're imprisoned by the enemy's crafty lies. What is sin? Sin is a choice to act on our will and not the Will of God. Sin itself doesn't make you do anything. You choose to commit sin. For example, you just don't fall into adultery. You've been tempted by someone, something (porn), or some way (social media). Your thinking lines with up with the sin and you become obsessed with repeated thoughts. You desire it. You then make a decision to act on the sin. Sin poisons the heart. It starts with a thought, motive, desire to create a vision in your imagination. A person dwells on the sin repetitively and eventually makes a move to sin. "The good person out of the good treasure of his heart produces good, and the evil person out of his evil treasure produces evil, for out of the abundance of the heart his mouth speaks." (Luke 6:45)

Life is in the blood, and God knows the heart. Man has never been able to replicate blood. Although, man has produced artificial hearts, arms, legs, and other prosthetics, the blood has to be transfused by donors. But this is not the pressing issue; it's that God looks at the thought life in the blood of the heart. Remember, the blood has a voice!

In the murder of Abel, the voice of the blood of Abel cried out in vengeance. It will speak either inside or outside the body. "The Lord saw that the wickedness of man was great in the earth, and that every intention of the thoughts of his heart was only evil continually." (Genesis 6:5) Our thoughts rule our hearts! God knew in the beginning that man would surely fall even after the flood:

> And when the Lord smelled the pleasing aroma, the Lord said in his heart, 'I will never again curse the ground because of man, for the intention of man's heart is evil from his youth. Neither will I ever again strike down every living creature as I have done. (Genesis 8:21)

Thoughts, intentions, and desires are all found in the hearts of men/women. We're warned to guard our hearts. "Keep thy heart with all diligence; for out of it are the issues of life." (Proverbs 4:23, KJV)

God wants us to be clean through the blood of Jesus. He wants us to come to Him and repent, which means to turn away from our sins. We need to run to the mercy seat of God and be clean. "Create in me a clean heart, O God, and renew a right spirit within me." (Psalm 51:10) When we make a decision to follow God, He can then renew our heart. "Therefore, if anyone in Christ, he is a new creation. The old has passed away; behold, the new has come." (2 Corinthians 5:17, ESV) Through the blood of Jesus, we have been redeemed of the sins of our past. This is your true eternal permanent birthday! In Christ alone, we can stand to take the crown of life in the next coming of Jesus. "Blessed is the man who remains steadfast under trial, for when he has stood the test, he will receive the crown of life, which God has promised to those who love him." (James 1:12) This is eternal life!

"By this love perfected with us, so that we may have confidence for the day of judgment, because as he is so also are we in this world." (1 John 4:17) Through the blood of Jesus, we can believe we're a part of His kingdom. "That they may all be one, just as you, Father, are in me, and I in you, that they also may be in us, so that the world may believe that you have sent me." (John 17:21)

Through the blood of Jesus, we can have mediation.

> And to the assembly of the firstborn who are
> enrolled in heaven, and to God, the judge of all,
> and to the spirits of the righteous made perfect,
> and to Jesus, the mediator of a new covenant, and
> to the sprinkled blood that speaks a better word
> than the blood of Abel. (Hebrews 12:23–24)

In contrast to Abel's blood, Jesus's blood cries out in holy, willingness mercy! Even when we don't know what to pray for, Jesus is always pleading out for us in heaven.

By our personal testimonies, we can sprinkle over the hearts of darkness a one-of-a-kind testimony; we have gone through and came out with Jesus on the other side. We have overcome the fiery darts of the enemy. Our testimony is how we show the world we are His. It's an individualized internal awakening to reassure us of our calling.

> Behold, I stand at the door and knock. If anyone hears my voice and opens the door, I will come in to him and eat with him, and he with me. The one who conquers, I will grant him to sit with me on my throne, as I also conquered and sat down with my Father on his throne. He who has an ear, let him hear what the Spirit says to the churches. (Revelation 3:20–22)

Through the blood of the Lamb and the power of our testimonies, we are signed, sealed, and delivered from our old selves. We're made brand-new with the sprinkling of the blood and our life experiences that led us from and back to God. We can have the confidence and assurance to walk in love and not hide anymore. We are to share the good news to all!

> The grace of the Lord Jesus be with all. Amen. (Revelation 22:21)
>
> But you will receive power when the Holy Spirit has come upon you, and you will be my witnesses in Jerusalem and in all Judea and Samaria, and to the end of the earth. (Acts 1:8)
>
> Go into all the world and proclaim the gospel to the whole creation. Whoever believes and is baptized will be saved, but whoever does not believe will be condemned. And these signs will accompany those who believe: in my name they will cast out demons; they will speak in new tongues; they will pick up serpents with their hands; and if they drink any deadly poison, it will not hurt them; they will lay their hands on the sick, and they will recover. (Mark 16:15–18)

Go therefore and make disciples of all nations, baptizing them in the name of the Father and of the Son and of the Holy Spirit, teaching them to observe all that I have commanded you. And behold, I am with you always, to the end of the age. (Matthew 28:19–20)

Spread the seeds of faith to produce these fruits. "But the fruit of the Spirit is love, joy, peace, patience, kindness, goodness, faithfulness, gentleness, self-control; against such things there is no law." (Galatians 5:22–23)

Note: Fruit of the Spirit: Joy

So God created man in his own image, in the image of God he created him; male and female he created them. (Genesis 1:27)

Then the Lord God formed the man from the dust of the ground and breathed into his nostrils the breath of life, and the man became a living being. (Genesis 2:7, NIV)

The Lord will fulfill his purpose for me; your steadfast love, O Lord, endures forever. Do not forsake the work of your hands. (Psalm 138:8)

O Lord, you have searched me and known me! You know when I sit down and when I rise up; you discern my thoughts from afar. You search out my path and my lying down and are acquainted with all my ways. Even before a word is on my tongue, behold, O Lord, you know it altogether. (Psalms 139:1–4)

For you formed my inward parts; you knitted me together in my mother's womb. I praise you, for I am fearfully and wonderfully made. Wonderful are your works; my soul knows it very well. My frame was not hidden from you, when I was being made in secret, intricately woven in the depths of the earth. Your eyes saw my unformed substance; in your book were written, every one of them, the days that were formed for me, when as yet there was none of them. (Psalms 139:13–16)

For I know the plans I have for you, declares the Lord, plans for welfare and not for evil, to give you a future and a hope. (Jeremiah 29:11)

Charm is deceitful, and beauty is vain, but a woman who fears the Lord is to be praised. (Proverbs 31:30)

So you also outwardly appear righteous to others, but within you are full of hypocrisy and lawlessness. (Matthew 23:28)

But what comes out of the mouth proceeds from the heart, and this defiles a person. For out of the heart come evil thoughts, murder, adultery, sexual immorality, theft, false witness, slander. (Matthew 15:18–19)

Do not judge by appearances, but judge with right judgment. (John 7:24)

Do you not know that you are God's temple and that God's Spirit dwells in you? (1 Corinthians 3:16)

And from those who seemed to be influential (what they were makes no difference to me; God shows no partiality)—those, I say, who seemed influential added nothing to me. (Galatians 2:6)

For in Christ Jesus you are all sons of God, through faith. For as many of you as were baptized into Christ have put on Christ. (Galatians 3:26–27)

Even as he chose us in him before the foundation of the world, that we should be holy and blameless before him. In love he predestined us for adoption to himself as sons through Jesus Christ, according to the purpose of his will, to the praise of his glorious grace, with which he has blessed us in the Beloved. (Ephesians 1:4–6)

For we are his workmanship, created in Christ Jesus for good works, which God prepared beforehand, that we should walk in them. (Ephesians 2:10)

And whatever you do, in word or deed, do everything in the name of the Lord Jesus, giving thanks to God the Father through him. (Colossians 3:17)

If you put these things before the brothers, you will be a good servant of Christ Jesus, being trained in the words of the faith and of the good doctrine that you have followed. Have nothing to do with irreverent, silly myths. Rather train yourself for godliness; for while bodily training is of some value, godliness is of value in every way, as it holds promise for the present life and also for the life to come. The saying is trustworthy and deserving of full acceptance. (1 Timothy 4:6–9)

Put on then, as God's chosen ones, holy and beloved, compassionate hearts, kindness, humility, meekness, and patience, bearing with one another and, if one has a complaint against another, forgiving each other; as the Lord has forgiven you, so you also must forgive. (Colossians 3:12–13)

For you are all children of light, children of the day. We are not of the night or of the darkness. (1 Thessalonians 5:5)

For physical training is of some value, but godliness (spiritual training) is of value in everything and in every way, since it holds promise for the present life and for the life to come. (1 Timothy 4:8, AMP)

But you are a chosen race, a royal priesthood, a holy nation, a people for his own possession, that you may proclaim the excellencies of him who called you out of darkness into his marvelous light. (1 Peter 2:9)

Your beauty should not come from outward adornment, such as elaborate hairstyles and the wearing of gold jewelry or fine clothes. Rather, it should be that of your inner self, the unfading beauty of a gentle and quiet spirit, which is of great worth in God's sight. (1 Peter 3:3–4, NIV)

See what kind of love the Father has given to us, that we should be called children of God; and so we are. The reason why the world does not know us is that it did not know him. (1 John 3:1)

About the Author

T ina D. Thompson was born and raised in the foothills of the Smoky Mountains of East Tennessee. Her great passions are Jesus Christ and her family. The Attack on Eve: God's Vision vs. World's Vision is her debut book.

CPSIA information can be obtained
at www.ICGtesting.com
Printed in the USA
LVHW031918190319
611200LV00001B/2